IMAGES
of America
COLTS NECK

MONMOUTH STAMP & COIN SHOP
39 Monmouth Street
Red Bank, New Jersey 07701
(732) 741-0626

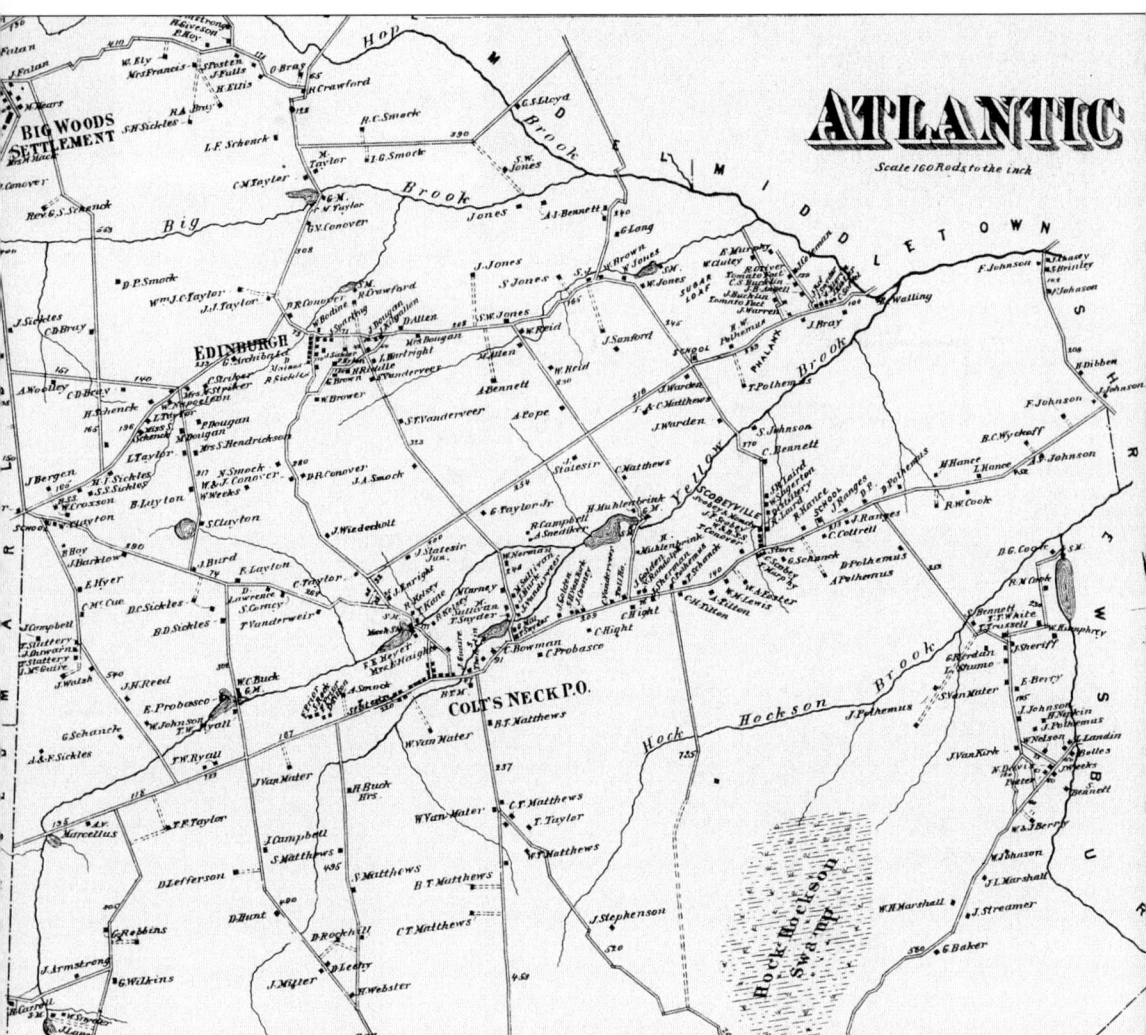

Plate 31 of the 1873 Beers Comstock and Cline *Atlas of Monmouth County* shows Colts Neck village virtually in the center of Atlantic Township. The two other settlements with the same size of type are Edinberg (its name later changed to Vanderberg) and Big Woods (the township's most obscure place name, but one referenced in the journal of at least one well-known traveler—Bishop Corrigan). Phalanx and Scobeyville, both former post towns, are depicted in small block letters. The area that became Earle is below Colts Neck, the white space reflecting its unpopulated state. Note the size then of Hockhockson Swamp. As this is being written in early May 1998 following 10 days of rain, one wonders how many wet basements are in the area.

IMAGES of America
COLTS NECK

Randall Gabrielan

Copyright © 1998 by Randall Gabrielan
ISBN 0-7524-0504-7

Published by Arcadia Publishing,
an imprint of Tempus Publishing, Inc.
2 Cumberland Street
Charleston, SC 29401

Printed in Great Britain.

Library of Congress Catalog Card Number: 98-86389

For all general information contact Arcadia Publishing at:
Telephone 843-853-2070
Fax 843-853-0044
E-Mail arcadia@charleston.net

For customer service and orders:
Toll-Free 1-888-313-BOOK

Visit us on the internet at http://www.arcadiaimages.com

This book is dedicated to my dear wife, Barbara Ann, who makes them possible. She is seen with the author at the St. Catharine's picnic in September 1997, photographed by Peter Fullen, who expressed satisfaction with the publication of an earlier image by taking this one with its offer "for next year's book."

Cover Photograph: See page 22.

Contents

Acknowledgments		6
Introduction		7
1.	Phalanx	9
2.	Laird's	27
3.	N.W.S. Earle	47
4.	Farms	65
5.	Organizations	89
6.	People, Places, Events	103

Acknowledgments

Two of the three single-subject chapters cover current, active organizations: Laird & Co. and Navel Weapons Station Earle, both of which were helpful in supplying both images and information. Special thanks to Lisa Laird Dunn and Larrie W. Laird of Laird's and Michael K. Brady, public affairs officer of Earle.

The third chapter, Phalanx, is well represented in a public, private, and family collection, holdings which make-up most of Chapter One. My thanks to the Monmouth County Historical Association, Glenn Vogel, and George Richdale for their outstanding images; thanks, too, to Dolores Hayden for permission to reproduce her diagram.

Regularly contributing collections were accessed early in this project, including the private holdings of distinguished collector John Rhody and the publicly available pictures of Photography Unlimited by Dorn's, 23A Wallace Street, Red Bank, NJ. A local collector, Michael F. Bremer, lent generously. Thanks to each.

Several longtime Colts Neck residents contributed. Two were especially helpful with their shared memories, as well as their images. Particular thanks goes to Arnold Conover and Dorothy Decher Gunther.

Many lenders joined the ranks of co-producers of this volume. My thanks to all, including Olga Boeckel, George Dittmar, Gail Hunton and the Monmouth County Parks System, Margaret "Peg" Jordan, W. Edmund Kemble, Helen Kozabo, Mr. and Mrs. Q.A. Shaw McKean Jr., Thomas Moog, Gina and William Pursley, Special Collections & Archives, Rutgers University Libraries, Robert A. Schoeffling, the Shrewsbury Historical Society, Garrett and Elizabeth Makin Thompson, and Walter Zimmerer.

INTRODUCTION

Colts Neck history can be viewed from at least three principal perspectives. First, it is a colonial-era village, a hot bed of contention in the Revolution. The name, dating at least to 1690, has seen much speculation over its origin. The author infers from an old map that it was a coined name, originated when several nearby places were named for animal "necks," with no special significance for its equine association and with no proof to the folklore passed to explain the name.

Colts Neck is also a rural township, formed from parts of Freehold, Middletown, and Shrewsbury; it was established as Atlantic Township in 1847, a period when large, "original" townships were divided throughout New Jersey. The new municipality was dotted with villages or small settlements, as depicted on the p. 2 map.

The township was renamed for its best-known part in 1962. Colts Neck is also a place that has undergone massive change in the past 30 years or so, an on-going process that has reshaped the landscape and transformed its population. One should not attempt to view current events in a historical perspective, but it can be said with confidence that more of permanent import has happened to Colts Neck in the past 30 years than in the prior 300.

Colts Neck's proximity to the pine barrens led to clashes in the Revolution with loyalist-refugee pine-robbers. It was home to Joshua Huddy, noted martyr, and site of post-Battle of Monmouth skirmishes. Michael Field was killed during one; his grave is preserved as a memorial.

Two of the three notable Colts Neck sites highlighted herein predated the formation of the township. The North American Phalanx, organized in 1843, was usually described, even after Atlantic Township was organized, as being "near Red Bank." It left its name on the map, Phalanx being a former post office, a neighborhood, and the present name of the former "Red Bank road." Chapter One embraces both the communal settlement, the latter occupancy of its land, and the surrounding community.

Laird's, with origins in the village, identified its locale for the Scobeyville section following its move after an 1849 fire. Their proud history as arguably the oldest business in Monmouth County is outlined in Chapter Two, which contains detail on the production of apple jack. Laird and Company is likely the only occupant keeping the Scobeyville place name current.

Naval Weapons Station Earle, founded in 1943 as Naval Ammunition Depot Earle, was located principally in Colts Neck because of the obscurity of the locale and the sparseness of the surrounding settlement. An initial announcement of the site's selection had its location wrong, the *Register* headline of July 1, 1943, claiming, "Navy To Take Over Shrewsbury Township." Earle's locale still causes confusion in Navy circles for a different reason. Other weapons stations embrace their municipal name, causing some to search for Earle on maps. Although the base appears as a map feature, Earle is not mapped as a place. Chapter Three depicts the why, how, and what of its creation.

Colts Neck is also a town of people, organizations, and historically significant farms. A representation is presented, as space and pictorial resources permitted, with the regrettable omission of many of the farms. Colts Neck was rural until the 1960s, containing a stock of old, significant farmhouses. Many of these productive farms were sold to urbanites as country estates, a transformation still evident on County Highway 537.

Suburbanization came later to Colts Neck than to other nearby communities. The first major developments, such as Clover Hill Estates, were built in the 1960s. Its houses were at the upper end of the market of the time, but were of a size and scale not unlike surrounding areas. The arrival of intensive development in the 1980s, an on-going process, brought a large number of houses of a size and scale overshadowing most of what had preceded them in Monmouth County. Their impact in demographic and social change is major, a current event of an import that can not be measured in a historic sense now, but one that makes a loud visual impact in so many recently quiet sections.

Many of Colts Neck's old fine structures have been lost in the massive building campaign. Preservation needs a higher profile in the township. One hopes the day does not arrive when the land is historically exhausted and barren, with residents wondering what made Colts Neck's past special.

This book was organized embracing a conscious decision to illustrate well Colts Neck's three foremost historical subjects, knowing gaps elsewhere would result. Omissions usually stem from an absence of images or space; in this instance, the latter was acute. One hopes other worthy subjects can be included in a second book, presuming the acceptance of this one. Most of the author's works reach subsequent volumes. Thus, the readership is encouraged to lend material for a follow-up work. Contact me at 71 Fish Hawk Drive, Middletown, New Jersey 07748, or at (732) 671-2645.

One

PHALANX

The North American Phalanx was founded in 1843 as a communal living association by Albert Brisbane, a young intellectual influenced in France by the socialist theories of Charles Fourier. Brisbane's advocacy of Fourierism resulted in about two dozen social experimental colonies in the 1840s. This image from the April 25, 1853 *Illustrated News* was taken from a drawing by T.W. Whitley.

Early residents settling in September 1843 lived in two farm houses on the site (at left), building during the winter of 1843–44 a 40-by-80-foot three-story residential hall. Families were housed on the first and second floors, while single men resided on the top floor. The image is a copy print by Andrew Coleman of his 1850 daguerreotype. (Collection Monmouth County Historical Association.)

Agriculture was to be a cornerstone of economic life at the Phalanx, the lack of farming experience of nearly all of its members notwithstanding. Fruits and vegetables were among their most successful products. The all-purpose label suggests their output. (Collection Monmouth County Historical Association.)

The Phalanstery, a three-story building with a broad piazza along the front, was built in 1847. An apartment wing was added in 1851–52; both structures are shown at right. (Collection Monmouth County Historical Association.)

These pigs at the Phalanx were photographed in the early 20th century, long after the cooperatives days. (Collection of Glenn Vogel.)

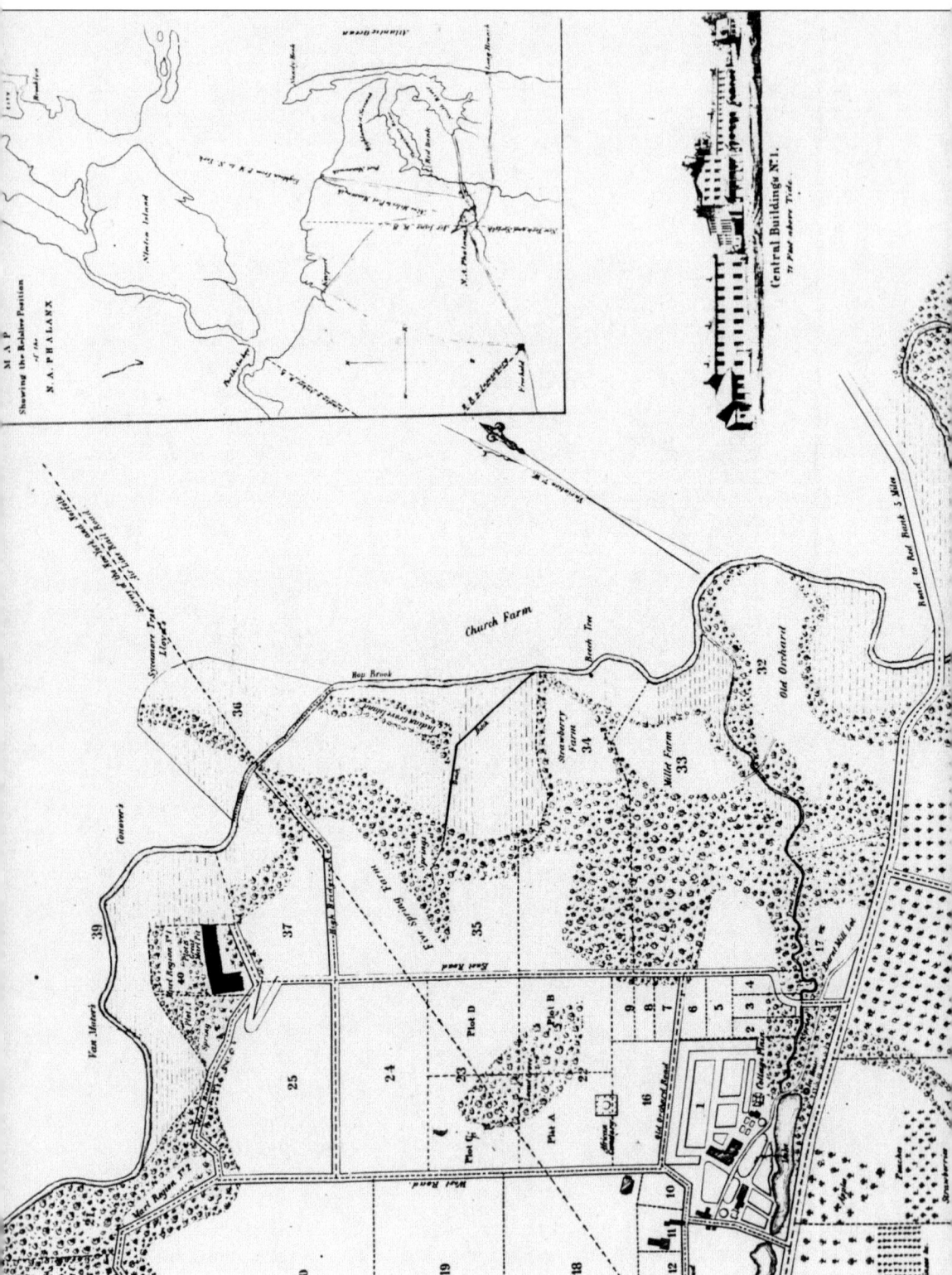

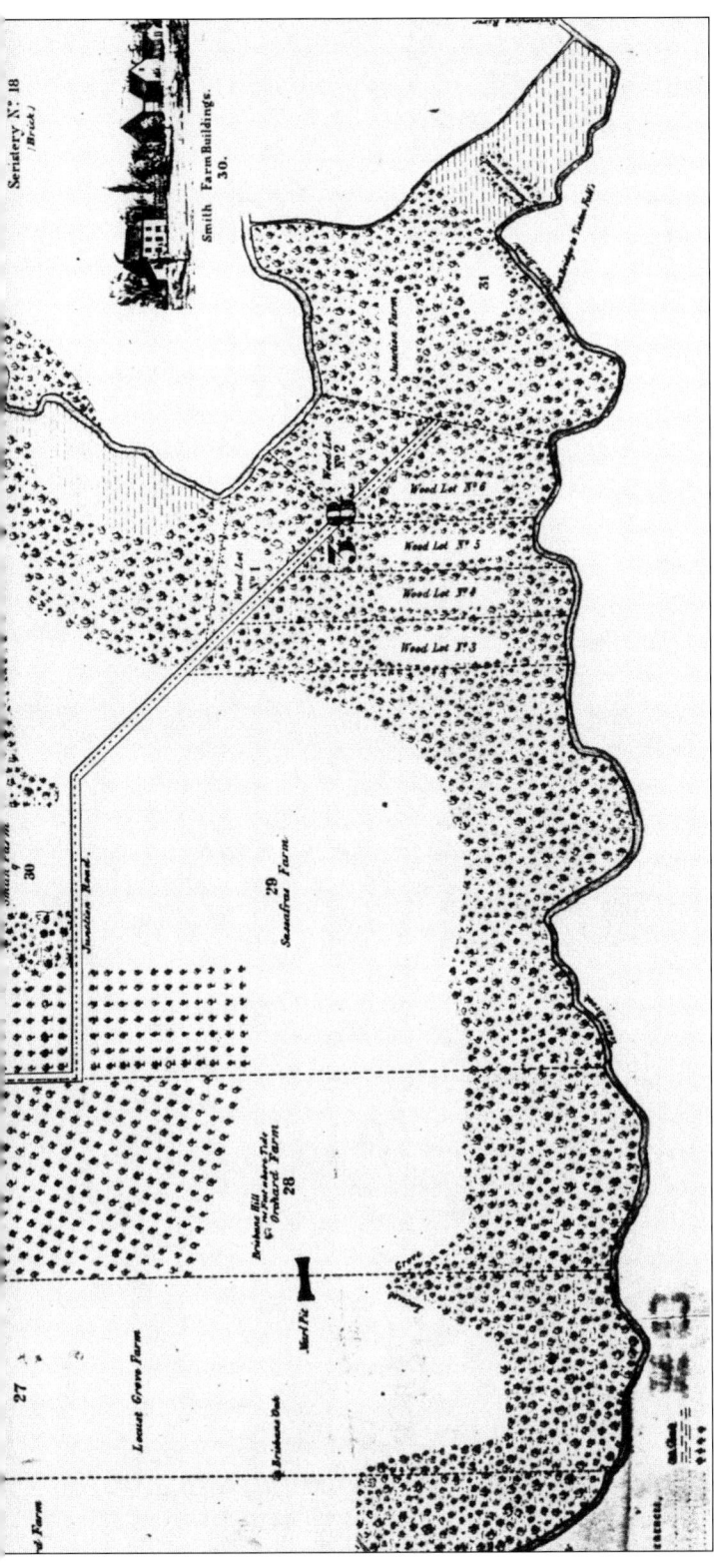

Phalanx founders bought about 600 acres bounded by the Hop and Yellow Brooks in 1843, the property bisected by what today is known as Phalanx Road. This map was issued in 1855 for the auction of the North American Phalanx property following the break-up of the organization. East of the stream was the Church Farm; much of it is the present location of Thompson Park and Brookdale Community College in Middletown Township. The main buildings were located on the bottom of this map, with the Phalanstery indicated as "no. 1." Note the existence of marl pits, the grainy material of decayed organic matter that was so valuable as fertilizer in the pre-chemical era.

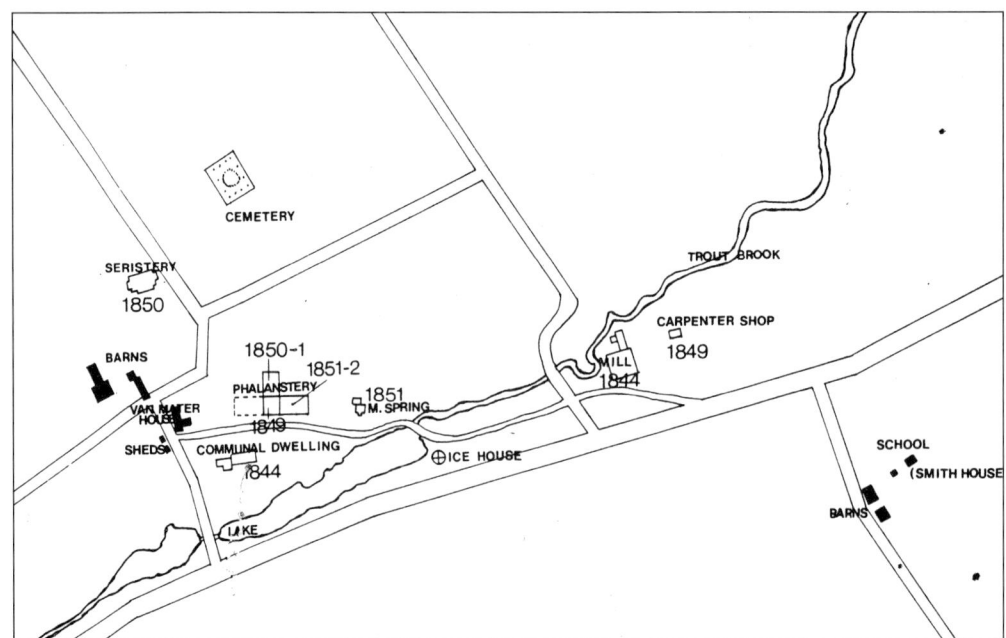

This diagram from Dolores Hayden's *Seven American Utopias* provides a helpful reference for the locations of several illustrated North American Phalanx structures. Phalanx Road runs across the image, while the two diagonal streets are Lovett Road (left) and Richdale Road. The two connected south of the cemetery by Bucklin Road. The solid images denote pre-1843 structures. The lake is now a stream flowing into the present Swimming River Reservoir.

The brick seristery, constructed in 1850, was the workshop of the fruit preserving group. It is depicted on the 1855 map drawn for the auction of the North American Phalanx property. (Collection Monmouth County Historical Association.)

The Marcus Spring cottage, described in the County's Historic Sites Inventory as one of the best examples of the Gothic Revival style in Monmouth County, was built in 1852 adjacent to the Phalanstery, as indicated on the diagram opposite. It was moved to the northwest corner of Bucklin and Richdale Roads. The board and batten clad house, distinguished by its steeply pitched gables, is built on a T-plan and features floor-to-ceiling windows on the first floor.

The Smith buildings, located on the south side of Phalanx Road as indicated on the diagram (top, opposite), were also depicted on the 1855 map. (Collection Monmouth County Historical Association.)

The view from the west suggests the size of the rear wing added to the Phalanstery. (Collection Monmouth County Historical Association.)

The Bucklin canning factory utilized the North American Phalanx seristery building (p. 14) and a long extension. This *c.* 1880s picture by Shear Bros. of Red Bank was probably taken for publicity or commemorative purposes as inferred by the appearance of what one presumes is the cannery staff.

This image of the south facade of the Phalanstery shows the building to its west, the Van Mater house according to the Hayden diagram. The image is from a c. 1910 photographic postcard. (Collection of Glenn Vogel.)

Noted critic and writer Alexander Woolcott was born at the Phalanx. The original photograph claims he is one of the subjects, pictured in front of the Phalanstery. (Special Collection & Archives, Rutgers University Libraries.)

Barn images are often unidentified, with their origins and departures infrequently documented. George Richdale believes this one, on Lovett Road, was demolished by the Lovetts in the 1950s. At least one substantial barn on the Phalanx antedated the community. It was claimed to be of mid-18th-century origin and one of finest examples of colonial carpentry in the county. It reportedly had 16-inch square oak posts and 16-by-24-inch cross beams. If so, the framing would have been nearly incombustible, but the barn was destroyed by fire in August 1920. (Special Collection & Archives, Rutgers University Libraries.)

This barn was near the present reservoir, about 200 feet behind a house east and north of Richdale and Bucklin Roads; George Richdale recalls it in dilapidated condition in the 1930s. The charcoal sketch is by William S. Bucklin, who was born 1851 at Phalanx and who studied at the Normal Art School, Boston, and with Frederick Roudel in New York. He was one of the first members of the Art Students League, and a member of the Greenwich Society and the Professional League of New York. His work includes paintings, murals, and stage curtains. Bucklin died at Phalanx in 1928. (Special Collections & Archives, Rutgers University Libraries.)

Foliage obscures a c. 1910 photographic postcard image of an unidentified Phalanx building. (Collection of Glenn Vogel.)

The original, undated but perhaps c. 1900, photograph describes the focal point as the Indian burial ground at Phalanx with Sugar Loaf in the distance. Sugar Loaf Hill is a promontory with a 199-foot elevation. A farm of that name, adjacent to the former North American Phalanx, was long-owned by the Polhemus family and consisted of 106 acres when Daniel McCormick sold the farm in 1937 to Ildon R. Blackburn for a country estate. (Collection Monmouth County Historical Association.)

The Bucklin canning plant is viewed early in this century with the receiving dock in the right background. Tomatoes were sent up a conveyor to large cooking vats on the second floor. (Collection of Michael F. Bremer.)

John Kubler reportedly bought 5 acres of North American Phalanx property near their former cannery then owned by Bucklin, and according to Mary B. Sim's *Commercial Canning in New Jersey/History and Early Development*, "built and put into operation his own canning factory in 1871. He canned tomatoes and string beans and raised on his own land most of what he canned." However, no buyer of that name was found in Monmouth County deeds. (Collection Monmouth County Historical Association.)

An unidentified Phalanx street on a c. 1910 photographic postcard depicts the area's wooded character and rough, narrow roads. (Collection of Glenn Vogel.)

The first Phalanx Post Office was established in February 1854. Emile Guillandon Jr. was postmaster, and the office remained open until December 1858. It was re-opened in June 1903, reflecting the local community use of the former cooperative's name, with George P. Bartle as postmaster. He is pictured here in 1913. (Collection of Glenn Vogel.)

The Richdale farm totaled in time about 63 acres around the Richdale family home, all planted in fruit. James C. Richdale is under the late-19th-century-barn's window. His son, George C., is standing to his left; he is the father of the lender of this c. 1920s image, also named George. Employee George Vernell is sitting at the door; the others are not identified. Richdale was a progressive farmer, an early advocate of spraying, who enhanced his yield greatly by chemical control of pests. He also sowed clover in the orchard, plowing it under for use as fertilizer. The orchards closed in 1951, but the barn still stands west of Richdale Road.

The Richdale orchard also grew peaches, including varieties no-longer marketed. Holding newly picked examples are Frank Richdale Jr. (left) and George Richdale Sr., flanking Peter Clark, the former's grandson.

Joe Zaleski, a Richdale employee, is seen in the 1920s using a grain drill, typically used at the time to plant oats, rye, or wheat seeds among existing plants.

Ethel Walling, born a Conover nearby in Lincroft, sketched in 1908 cow barns once part of the Richdale farm. George Richdale recalls they were located near the present reservoir and collapsed after a lengthy period of disuse.

What little evidence of the village of Phalanx that remains is embodied by a row of three houses on the north side of Phalanx Road, east of Richdale Avenue, numbers 265 (left), 267 (center), and 269. One contained the former post office. They are still recognizable, this c. 1915 image altered by minor modifications and, as respects the latter building, repair of fire damage.

The Phalanx had fallen on hard times by the mid-20th century. The Phalanstery had been an apartment house and housed migrant farm workers in the World War II period, a time when the tomato canning plant was reactivated. Plans to continue the tomato operation failed; a tax sale auction reflected the property's dismal commercial prospects. The Phalanx's historic stature attracted preservation interests, however.

Recognition of the national significance of the Phalanx was sparked by the research of architectural historian Dolores Hayden, who had undertaken a major study of cooperative communities in America. The Colts Neck Historical Society, which had organized a "Save the Phalanx" effort, had its offer of $40,000 rejected by the owners. The place was destroyed by fire on November 14, 1972.

The building was unoccupied and without electricity when the "suspicious" fire broke out. An alarm was sounded at about 11:00 p.m., the blaze burning out of control past 1:30 a.m.. Blowing sparks and embers from the "spectacular" fire threatened nearby properties. About 24 engines from fire companies in Colts Neck and surrounding towns, including the Earle base, fought the blaze.

Firemen, hampered by inadequate water, laid nearly 2 miles of hose, using water from nearby streams. They managed to save a portion of the eastern wing, which had contained family apartments. The remaining structure was not viable and was later demolished. Nothing remains today, with new private houses built around the site.

Old trees remain in the Phalanx area, as evidenced by this pruning scene in the summer of 1976.

Two

LAIRD'S

William Laird settled in Monmouth County from Scotland by 1698 and is believed to have produced apple jack at least since then. A Laird ancestor built the Colts Neck Inn in 1717 (see p. 104); apple jack and apple brandy have always been best sellers there. The firm's records trace the earliest commercial production of apple jack to 1780 at this location. A gallon of "cyder spirits," as apple jack was called, cost four shillings, six pence in the 18th century.

Production continued at the Colts Neck Inn site until 1849, when the distillery was destroyed by fire. The second Robert Laird, son of Samuel, moved apple jack operations to the Scobeyville site, where the business continues today. James Laird is pictured c. 1880 at left with Joseph Tilton Laird Sr. The latter was a jockey in his younger years, riding the famed horse Fashion in the early 1840s. (The Laird's Collection.)

Laird's occupies the former Capt. Scobey house as an office; it is located on the north side of County Highway 537, at Laird Road. The earlier part of the house was built c. third quarter of the 18th century. The place was remodeled for office use in 1934. (The Laird's Collection.)

Laird's has never grown apples, but buys large quantities from orchards. Only select, tree-ripened apples are used in making apple jack; thus, pressing into juice is done at harvest time from early September to mid-November. It takes 16 pounds of apples to make one 750 milliliter bottle of straight apple brandy, while 100 pounds of apples are required to make one proof gallon (i.e. 100 proof) of brandy. This delivery image dates from the early 1950s. (The Laird's Collection.)

Eating, as opposed to drinking, apples appeared to be a novel idea in the mid-19th century. The *Monmouth Democrat* of April 25, 1850, quoted the *American Agriculturist's* advocating the healthfulness of their use as food. There were cultural issues, as their examples of salubrious consumption were European. Economics of marketing was a factor, as heavy, inexpensive apples likely could not be shipped to distant markets profitably. However, they could strengthen rural laborers and even replace the desire for animal flesh, according to their very enthusiastic advocates. (The Laird's Collection.)

Robert Laird is pictured c. late 19th century behind the fence in front of the original Laird Scobeyville office, which was built in 1851.

The original cider mill is viewed in a late-19th-century image. Robert Laird served under Washington in the Revolution. The Laird family supplied the troops with apple jack when they were in the Monmouth area.

A former power plant is viewed in a late-19th-century image. The 1851 facility still stands north of the modern plant. These old survivors of an important early industry have been designated as eligible for listing in the National Register of Historic Places.

The 1851 office showed little exterior change in the 1950s; it was converted to a laboratory after repeal. At left is the old cooper's shop, standing in front of the 1850s warehouse. (The Laird's Collection.)

Washed apples are being conveyed by water to the grinder to be ground into a wet pomace. Apples with high sugar content, such as the winesap, are preferred. John E. Laird, president in 1936, when announcing a contest for developing a new apple highly suited for apple jack, commented that he believed most of the 3,000 recognized varieties of apples grown in the United States had been tried. Fruit lovers are poorer for most of those varieties having fallen out of cultivation. (The Laird's Collection.)

A hydraulic apple press presses juice from wet pomace, straining it through cheese cloth to remove solids. The juice was then pumped to fermentation tanks. (The Laird's Collection.)

Crushed juice ferments from 7 to 30 days, with colder weather lengthening the fermentation process. These 20,000-gallon wood fermentation tanks, viewed in Scobeyville in 1959, were removed in the 1970s; some were relocated at the North Garden, Virginia plant, the present manufacturing facility. (The Laird's Collection.)

Fermented juice contains about 12% alcohol. Timing the fermentation process is critical, as cider fermenting too long turns to vinegar. (The Laird's Collection.)

Fifty-gallon charred oak barrels used once for bourbon are viewed on 1934 wood storage racks. Apple jack is stored a minimum of four years; apple brandy storage is about 7 years, with the aging product improving at the risk of evaporation. The Laird storage facility can hold the product of 20,000 tons of apples (The Laird's Collection.)

Barrels are being emptied, or "dumped" in industry parlance, over a screened trough which catches any charcoal. The bung on a barrel's side is placed on the bottom when emptied, with the bung hole lined with cheese cloth. John Ward is overseeing the process in the early 1980s. (The Laird's Collection.)

Distilled apple jack is passed through a "try box," permitting quality control experts to check proof, temperature, and clarity of the apple jack. Proof is monitored frequently after distillation. (The Laird's Collection.)

> "Each year shall give this apple-jack
> A mellower taste, a warmer bloom,
> A potency 'gainst mopes and gloom,
> And make it, when the frost-clouds lower,
> A thing for punch of wondrous power.
> The years shall come and pass, but we
> Shall grow no better where we lie,
> While summer's songs and autumn's sigh
> Shall ripen the apple-jack."

The verse is from *The Drinking of the Apple Jack* by George Arnold, the poet of the Phalanx; its versification was a parody of William Cullen Bryant's great poem of nature, *The Planting of the Apple Tree*. Some of the rhymes are even identical. (The Laird's Collection.)

A fermentation tank with lines to a feed tank is viewed in front of the World War II-era apple pomace dehydration building used for the manufacture of pectin, a product used to jell foods and drugs. In addition, a newly acquired plant in Lyons, New York, produced for the war effort cider vinegar, used to pickle and preserve foods sent overseas. (The Laird's Collection.)

The apple selection along with close control of the natural fermentation period and the distillation process are important to the quality and flavor of the finished apple jack. (The Laird's Collection.)

Fermented juice, or hard cider, is double distilled in pot stills. The first distillation raises the proof to 80, or 40% alcohol by volume; the second distillation raises the brandy to 160 proof, or 80% alcohol. The brandy is then reduced to 130 proof, the ideal for the aging process in 50-gallon charred oak barrels. (The Laird's Collection.)

A column still, the bottom of one installed c. 1969, is seen here. It contains a rectifying column which raises the proof of apple brandy to 165, at which point it is reduced in a receiving tank to 130, prior to placement in charcoaled oak barrels purchased from a whiskey distiller. This equipment is inactive, having served until 1976. (The Laird's Collection.)

The teenage Larrie Laird, now president of the company, is seen *c.* 1959 in front of a low wine still, also known as a beer still, which produces low proof brandy in the first distilling process. He is of the eighth generation of the family to run the business, arguably Monmouth's oldest. (Special Collection and Archives, Rutgers University Libraries.)

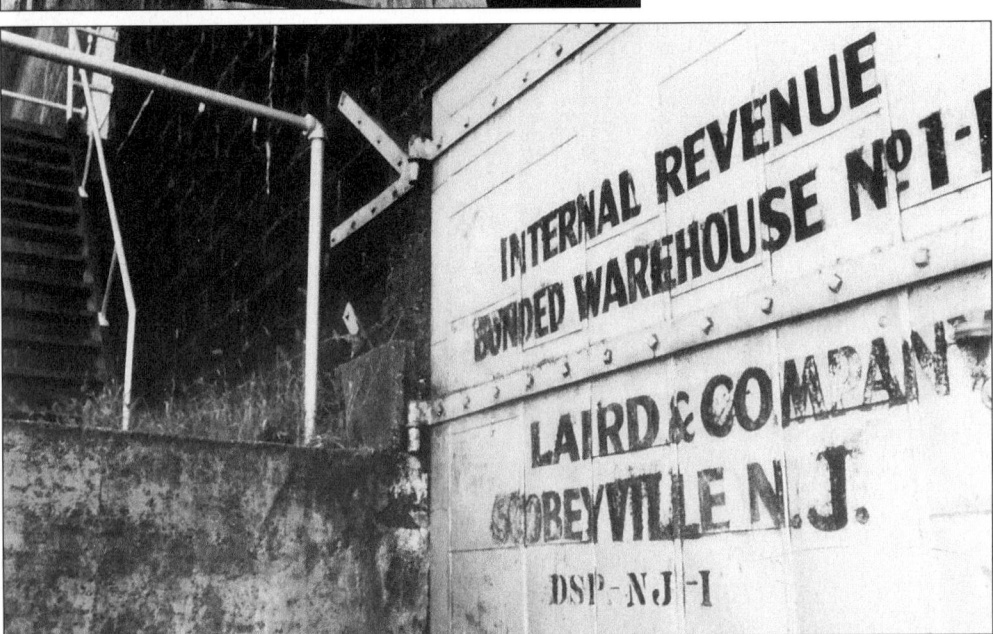

The door to the barrel warehouse reflects its status as a bonded facility, which means that its contents have been determined as taxable, rather than tax having been paid. The taxing process is simpler now than in the time when tax stamps had to be purchased prior to bottling and placed on each bottle. Note the license number, indicating Laird's status as the first licensed bottler of distilled spirits following repeal of Prohibition. (The Laird's Collection.)

President Larrie Laird posed over a barrel in the 1980s, perhaps demonstrating the process of taking out a bung for testing. (The Laird's Collection.)

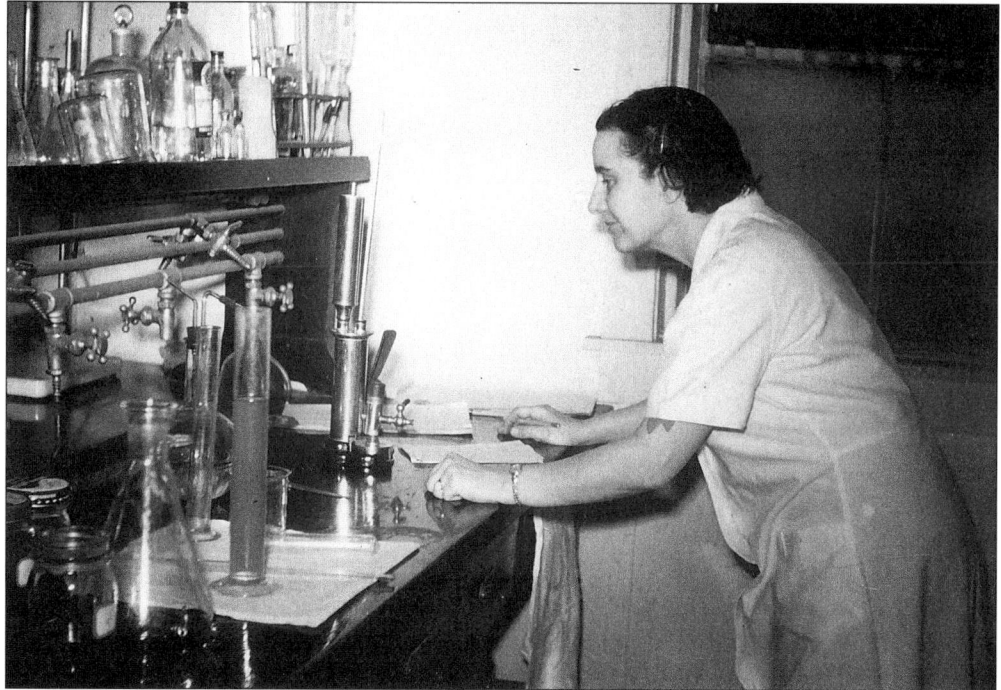

Andree Maver is engaged in the proofing process in the old lab, now vacant. The steel ebuliometer tests the percentage of alcohol in the juice. A saccerameter is inside the beaker, a device for testing sugar content. The image is from the 1950s. (The Laird's Collection.)

This bottle filler, viewed in November 1974, is still in use. The machine first vacuums air from the bottle, and ascertains if a hole exists in it. (The Laird's Collection.)

This inspection spot in a late 1950s line is checking for proper filling, affixing of label, and placement of tax stamp. Two of the inspectors have been identified as Helen Dobry (left) and Peggy Mauser (right). (The Laird's Collection.)

The production line in the late 1950s required placement of Federal tax stamps on each bottle, a step eliminated by current tax collection procedure. Annie Mauser (left), is affixing the stamps, as Peggy Mauser prepares to do so. (The Laird's Collection.)

The production of the 1,000,000th case since repeal of Laird's apple brandy was the cause for celebration at the plant in the spring of 1951. John Evans Laird holds the bottle proudly. To his right are Earl Reed, who ran the production line, and Mary Oryll. At right is Clarence Willett; the others remain unidentified. Employees were given a silver dollar for each year of service at the party that followed. (The Dorn's Collection.)

Paul, a government officer, intently watches the regauge process for tax determination, while John Thompson waits in front of the barrel in a 1950s scene. (The Laird's Collection.)

John Thompson is moving a barrel off the scale, as Walter Woolley has his back to the camera in the 1950s. (The Laird's Collection.)

Older labels were colorful graphically and could invoke colorful viewer responses. The private label bottling for the Schulte stores suggests the beverage's rustic origins and country favor. Jersey Lightnin' is a traditional colloquial name for apple jack, suggesting warmth and power. A 1936 news item indicated the brand name and packaging was a competitive response to lower-priced whiskeys. However, Lairds believes the label was produced only to register the trademark to preclude others from using the name. (The Laird's Collection.)

Walter Woolley (left) and John Evans Laird Jr. are engaged in the organoleptic process, or the testing of product by look, smell, and taste. They are in the lab c. mid-1950s. (The Laird's Collection.)

Modern facilities have been built around the 1850s structures, with several of the latter still standing, unused, around the large complex. An inactive scale house and the cider mill in the rear of this 1980s image are two such structures. (The Laird's Collection.)

Laird & Co. remodeled and refurbished the old Capt. Scobey house for office use in 1934, also making a major Colonial Revival expansion on the west. J. Hallam Conover of Freehold, the county's leading architect of that style during the height of the Colonial Revival and into the 1950s, used 18th-century Monmouth County structures as his design inspiration. The building—the south facade is seen here—is little changed since its erection. Fireplace tilework illustrating apple brandy production is one of the interior decorative highlights.

Mabel Laird (Mrs. John Evans Laird Sr.), mother of the present president, Larrie, is viewing ancient company records in 1959. The firm cultivates its proud history, including records such as George Washington's requesting the recipe for apple jack. Laird history is an integral part of their 1992 Apple Jack Cookbook, *Apple Jack: The Spirit of America*. (William Augustine Collection, Special Collections & Archives, Rutgers University Libraries.)

The Laird's plant is seen *c.* 1970 after completion of the large bottling building. The view is north from County Highway 537, just west of Laird Road. The office on the opposite page is in the foreground, while some old buildings can be seen at left. (The Laird's Collection.)

This June 1981 aerial reflects the addition of a warehouse to the right of the bottling plant, as seen on the previous page, a view unchanged today. The body of water at top is the Swimming River Reservoir, just south of the dam, the outlet of Yellow Brook, which runs through the Laird property. Laird today bottles a variety of distilled spirits, both under its own name and for private labels. (The Laird's Collection.)

Lisa Laird Dunn, Larrie W. Laird, and John E. Laird III, holding the inflatable "bottle," show-off part of the corporate collection. Laird's Apple Jack has been filled over the years in a variety of bottles, jugs, and commemorative flasks; those pictured in the late 1980s represent only part of the collection, which also contains art work, and, as must be obvious now, quite a few photographs. (The Laird's Collection.)

46

Three
N.W.S Earle

The federal government, when seeking a site for a munitions depot during World War II, wanted one near New York Harbor, but located in a sparsely settled area in order to reduce the potential harm of accidents and to improve security. The site that became Earle was preferred over others considered. Most of its interior was in rural Atlantic Township, while smaller parts were in Shrewsbury Township (the future Borough of Tinton Falls) and Howell Township. The first Navy office was in the Red Funnels, a roadhouse acquired with the Atlantic site. The security fence indicates the image is post-Navy ownership, but it is also dated—December 13, 1943.

The base's first commanding officer, Capt. Burton H. Green, placed his personal imprint on the facility, guiding work with his motto, "Our primary purpose is to furnish ammunition to the fleet; all else is secondary." The base, however, was named for Rear Admiral Ralph Earle, born 1874 in Worcester, Massachusetts. Earle was an 1896 graduate of the United States Naval Academy. He was decorated for valor in the Spanish-American War, became a specialist in ordnance, and rose to be chief of the Bureau of Ordnance of the Navy and commander of the Naval Proving Ground at Indianhead. Earle went to sea after World War I, commanded the battleship *Connecticut* and resigned in 1925 to become president of Worcester Polytechnic Institute, a position he held at his death in 1939. (Official US Navy photograph.)

A 65-foot steel watch tower, 16 feet square at its base (which was built on concrete piers), was erected in 1924 on Signal Hill. The tower, ascended by criss-crossed flights of stairs, narrowed to 12 feet square at its peak where a room for a watchman was placed. Arnold Conover recalls quite a few fires in the area during his youth and youngsters being impressed into firefighting duty. This is a 1952 image of the mobile mine assembly area; presumably it is the original tower in the background. The watch tower was removed at an unknown date; a water tower and radio antenna are on the site now. (Official US Navy photograph.)

The *Red Bank Register* reported on March 23, 1910, that the Securities Development Company was offering 25-by-100-foot lots on former Haight estate property along Asbury Avenue in a southeast section of the township known as the "scrub oak district." The tree grew profusely in an area partly sandy and partly marshy that had been selling for $2 an acre not many years earlier for buyers willing to risk a "long shot investment." The woodland lots were selling for $10 to $50 per lot in 1910. This *c.* late 1940s image captures both sandy and wooded land. (Official US Navy photograph.)

According to a 25-year retrospective in the October 16, 1968 *The Earle Missile*, the first piece of earth moving equipment began work on August 2, 1943. Terrain impacted the project as "a furious four day rain completely filled in excavations for buildings, and sank derricks and barges." This image is c. late 1940s, probably taken for erosion study, showing the present inert storage area, a place originally used for ordnance renovation work. (Official US Navy photograph.)

This small house appears typical of the 1910 decade, a reminder that the Earle property, although sparsely settled, had a number of residents. The building, seen in a 1952 image, was in the administrative-industrial area and was taken down at an unknown date. In its later years, the house was surrounded by the Navy's new railroad and a World War II-era Quonset hut. (Official US Navy photograph.)

Initial construction of essential facilities was immediate and rapid beginning in 1943. The base has been virtually a continual construction project for upgrade and expansion of facilities. This image shows the early 1950s expansion of a C 2 area administrative building. (Official US Navy photograph.)

Initial news articles about the base had an alarming tone. The first *Register* headline, although inaccurate as to locale, "Navy To Take Over Shrewsbury Township," set a pattern of expressing concern for the future of the land. The next week's outlined a practical matter, "Calls Attention to Grade Crossing Danger." The paper also contained a letter from Edgar O. Murphy, freeholder director, to the Navy requesting overpasses at busy intersections. This May 31, 1944 aerial shows a little-changed scene at the County Highway 537 overpass. Overpasses were also built over the railroads, Highways 36 and 35, Leonardville Road, and County Highway 520 (Newman Springs Road). (Official US Navy photograph.)

This construction scene appears to be the mobile mine assembly unit on Signal Hill, a site where mines are assembled and fuzed, or disarmed if returned from the fleet unused. The excavation is likely protection against explosion. (Official US Navy photograph.)

The Command Administration Building (C-2) is located at the north end of Kula Road, a short distance from Earle's major east-west thoroughfare, Esperance Road, which begins at Highway 34. The T-shaped structure was part of the initial base construction. Anti-aircraft guns decorate the lawn.

Housing for non-commissioned officers and their families south of the main gate and Esperance Road is viewed in a 1982 image. The area, recently remodeled, is named Green Acres in honor of Capt. Burton H. Green, the base's founding commanding officer.

Pam, Jim, & Christopher Brian lived in 607-B Blandy Road (seen above, near house on Right) from August 1997 through May 1999. Jim was a family physician at

The base is viewed in 1951 north of Esperance Road, the main road running east from the Highway 34 gate. Saipan Road is the north-south street bisecting the picture. The rail yard and round house are in the upper right, beyond the long, end-gabled building with the light roof, a supply warehouse. The public works department and gym are two occupants of the large structure at left center, while the twin building at left rear functions for automobile storage and fleet support. A number of the buildings have been altered and an athletic field was developed in the left foreground. (Official US Navy photograph.)

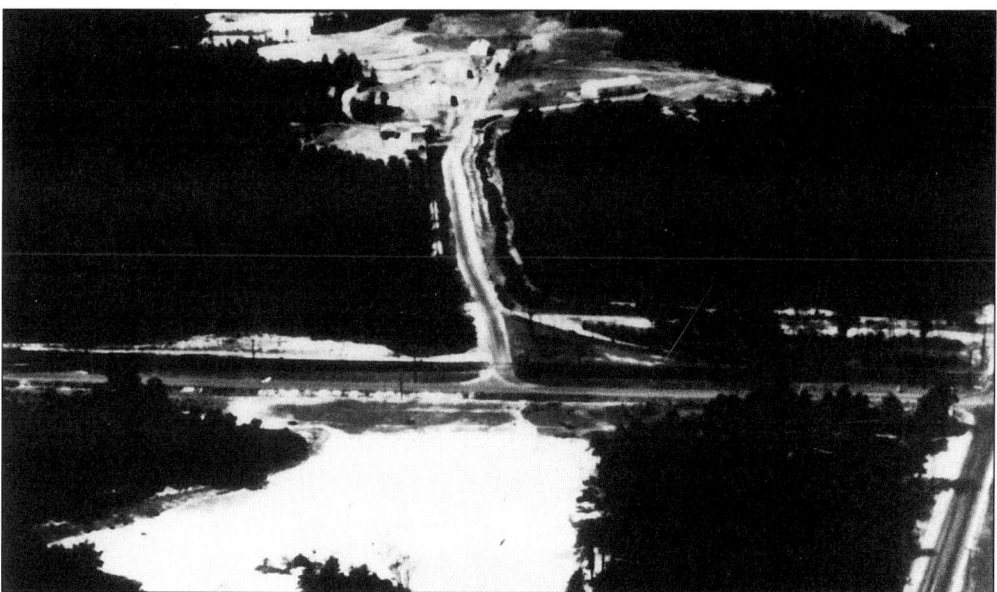

A glimpse of "back of the base" operations is seen c. 1950. The beginning of Normandy Road is at right, while Midway Road crosses the picture. The light area at bottom was once used to demilitarize ordnance. An incinerator was once located here to burn unneeded weapons materials, an operation now removed. The inert storage area is the light area at top with the small round structures. It warehouses non-explosive materials for weaponry. (Official US Navy photograph.)

Branch Medical Clinic NWS Earle (Building C-3) From August 1997 until June 2001. From Nov 2000 → June 2001 Jim worked at BMC Mechanicsburg PA (Temp. duty). Pam & Jim & Christopher moved to Hummelstown PA in May A99.

New officer housing quarters are seen in a January 1947 image; three similar structures were built. (Official US Navy photograph.)

Buildings have also been moved as part of Earle's long-term construction process. Building J-106, Wing A (foreground) and Wing B (in the rear), are viewed at their new locations in April 1948 in one of Earle's magazine areas. (Official US Navy photograph.)

Normandy Road, Earle's private road from the inland base to the pier, crosses the Swimming River, the border between Middletown and Tinton Falls, east of the reservoir dam on Swimming River Road. The view is west—the railroad runs north-south at this point—prior to the construction of the present road, which is adjacent to the rail line. In addition, the trestle has been filled-in with earth. The picture, although undated, is early as mature vegetation has also changed the landscape. (Official US Navy photograph.)

This 1955 image is a Mighty Mouse mower shredder starting up the slope of the north side of a magazine. Grass cutting, contracted-out now, is performed with heavier motorized equipment. (Official US Navy photograph.)

The fire company is part of Naval Weapons Station Earle's Security Department, which embraces law enforcement, escort, and guard monitoring, as well as visitor control (such as authors borrowing pictures). The Earle fire forces, consisting of about 42 personnel at two fire houses (one inland and one in Leonardo), is one of only two full-time, paid departments in Monmouth County on duty 24 hours a day; the other is Fort Monmouth's. The tractor has been replaced since this c. 1980s image was taken, but the tank is still in service. Earle also maintains an aerial truck and a variety of other specialized vehicles, including water rescue and rough terrain vehicles.(Official US Navy photograph.)

Earle fire fighters have assisted nearby municipal departments in times of need. Their fire prevention activities include controlled burns to reduce the quantity of dry vegetation which could pose a fire threat. This c. 1950s example is an actual fire rather than a drill. (Official US Navy photograph.)

Earle first celebrated Armed Forces Day on May 20, 1950, opening several buildings including the fire house, barracks, the sick bay, storage and repair garages, and various shops. The visitors were also taken to ammunition igloos. This c. late 1950s image shows a Marine tank believed to be in an Armed Forces Day exercise. (Official US Navy photograph.)

A crowd at an unidentified Armed Forces Day is seen inspecting a Terrier missile, perhaps c. late 1950s. The Terrier, developed c. 1950, was an early missile system that had a long life through regular upgrades. This example is from the BT-3 family of ship-to-shore or ship-to-ship missiles. Celebration of the day has waned and the base is no longer open then. However, Earle has an equivalent open house, its Summerfest, occurring in each June. (Official US Navy photograph.)

A magazine built into the side of a hill reduced the potential for damage in the event of an accident. The image is c. 1950s. (Official US Navy photograph.)

Single-arch magazines of reinforced concrete, called igloos, were built in World War II. The mounds included 6 feet of earth at the base, tapering to 2 feet at top, a design that minimized the potential for an explosion to spread, as it directed the force upward. (Official US Navy photograph.)

The single-arch igloos designed for World War II-era ammunition could be a tight fit for the rockets and missiles employed in the Cold War era, as evidenced by this c. 1950s image. (Official US Navy photograph.)

This c. 1950s image depicts the limited storage capacity of smaller igloos for larger ordnance. Later igloos, typically built in units of three, were larger. (Official US Navy photograph.)

A three-unit igloo magazine, known as a triple arch, is viewed in a 1980s image. Earle is now free of nuclear weapons. United States policy is not to comment on the locale of nuclear arms; the conclusion was reached by nuclear arms experts, who use among their evidence the presence or absence of special Marine guard detachments whose only assignment is protection of nuclear weapons. (Official US Navy photograph.)

This undated image of one of about 12 magazine groups built throughout the base. The long magazine in the center is a c. 1980 design intended to store missiles. (Official US Navy photograph.)

An employee is engaged in the renovating process on 5-inch shells to assure their continued reliability. The shells are banded together to prevent their tipping in transit. The image is late 1960s. (Official US Navy photograph.)

The Earle transfer depot is seen in an undated image. Some magazines are accessible only by truck, others only by rail. The transfer depot, dating from Earle's beginnings, permits transfer of material from one means of transport to the other. (Official US Navy photograph.)

The Earle railroad is a major freight-moving link between the inland storage base and the waterfront shipping point. It runs five locomotives and owns about 330 pieces of rolling stock. The road consists of 128 miles of track. It contains 60 barricades, each able to store four cars (for protection while awaiting unloading). (Official US Navy photograph.)

This 1982 image is of the railroad marshaling yard at the Colts Neck end of Normandy Road. Cars are carefully sorted and arranged to reach the pier in the correct order. The Navy minimizes the presence of loaded cars at the Leonardo section of the base; its storage facilities there are literally carved into a mountain.

The quantity of rolling stock varies with the level of activity at Earle. The base's public works department is proud of its well-equipped railroad roundhouse capable of locomotive overhaul. (Official US Navy photograph.)

A partially loaded container is viewed at an unspecified date. Railroad traffic varies with base activity. Typically during less-active times a train will go to the pier in the morning and return to Colts Neck in the evening. One can live close to a grade crossing and not see a Navy train for years. The protection of cargo varies with its make-up. Occasions when crossings were protected by armed sentries with helicopters overhead and armed gun-mounted escort vehicles led many observers to believe ordnance more potent than gun shells was being transported. (Official US Navy photograph.)

This 1960s image of a missile ready for delivery provides an example of protective packaging designed to promote safe handling and shipment. (Official US Navy photograph.)

A missile is seen onboard a ship at the Leonardo pier. The pier, built in 1943–44, was expanded later, and extends 2.2 miles into Sandy Hook Bay from the edge of the water to the end of the longest pier. Leonardo was desirable as a shipping point due to its proximity to the harbor at New York without presenting the congestion and population surrounding the prior dock at Jersey City. (Official US Navy photograph.)

Four
FARMS

One could usually prompt a listener's disbelief by claiming the ability to find a camel in Colts Neck. At least one resided on a Laird Road farm along with other animals exotic to the area, employed for use in advertising and stage work. The business was relocated to Orange County, New York c. 1990.

Big Brook Farm was one of Colts Neck largest and most historic farms. It is seen here in an aerial view from the early 1950s. Its 19th-century history is associated with the Taylor family. The Doug Taylor farm (one of the six that composed Big Brook) was home in the 1850s and '60s to a famed herd of South Down sheep, considered the best breed in the country, with Taylor sales going to virtually every state in the Union.

The main house of Big Brook stood at its Conover Road entrance.

Chrineyonce Conover, seen here in the cold storage building, was long the superintendent at Big Brook. Such facilities were unusual on local farms; this one had a capacity of 18,000 bushels.

Arnold Conover, born in Red Bank, was raised on Hockhockson and Brookside Farms in Colts Neck. A member of the first graduating class of the new Atlantic Township Elementary School (see p. 100), he went on to attend high school in Red Bank. He is seen here c. 1938 when working on Big Brook Farm's game preserve, which Frederick Burghard established for paying hunter-guests.

Walter C. Zimmerer Jr., born on May 30, 1918, and raised in Nutley, NJ, discovered Colts Neck by accident while visiting nearby. His agrarian instincts may have stemmed from helping on the farm of his grandfather, a German immigrant. In 1949 he bought Big Brook, an assemblage of 6 farms totaling 611 acres, a holding Zimmerer increased to 850. Zimmerer began an extensive local building career and raised Angus cattle, his herd numbering 500 head at one time. The Township Committee gave him the Outstanding Citizen Award in 1972, while 1983 brought him the Historic Angus Herd Award.

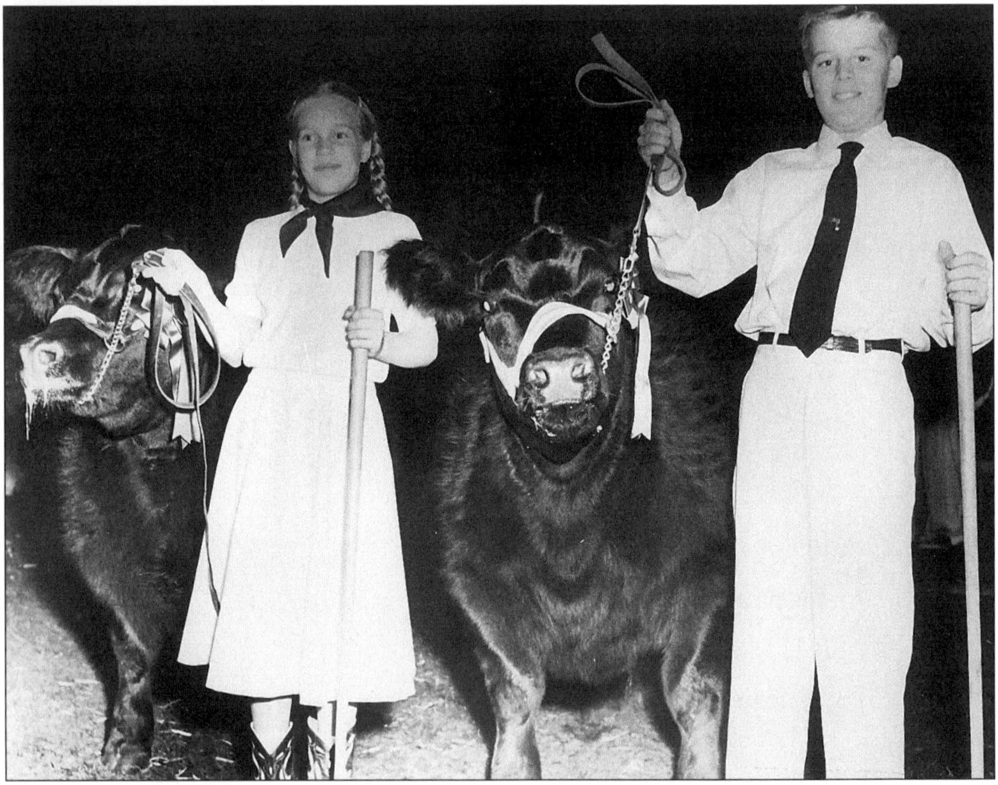

Zimmerer raised prize herds and also took pride in the 4H accomplishments of his children, who purchased cattle at market price after weaning, keeping track of their costs and time spent. Maryann and Walter Zimmerer III are shown here *c*. 1953 at an exhibition, after which the cattle were sold for slaughter. Champions brought better prices. Zimmerer still has an interest in cattle in Iowa.

The driveway from Conover Road to the interior of Big Brook Farm is depicted here in an early 1950s image. Apple orchards of older varieties comprised 125 acres of the initial purchase; Zimmerer planted an additional 100 acres in currently popular varieties. His construction began gradually—1, 7, and 17 houses in the first three years, but at a pace of 40–50 houses a year after that.

Walter Zimmerer built this house, seen in a c. 1951 aerial, on a Big Brook Farm hill. He still resides here with his wife, Erma, on a remaining 40 acres. His construction record numbers 28 subdivisions between Colts Neck and Holmdel. About his accidental discovery, Walter recalls, "It was the best trip I ever made. My wife and I love Colts Neck."

The mill on Bucks Mill Road was built in 1854 by Joseph Probasco, replacing an earlier structure on the site. The multi-storied, front-gabled building has the classic look of a gristmill, but this one at four stories and with a peanut stone foundation 2 feet thick and 20 feet deep was one of the most substantial, larger than any other structure in the area. It was erected by Abram "Boss Abe" Cottrell of Matawan at a time when milling still thrived in the area. (Special Collections & Archives, Rutgers University Libraries.)

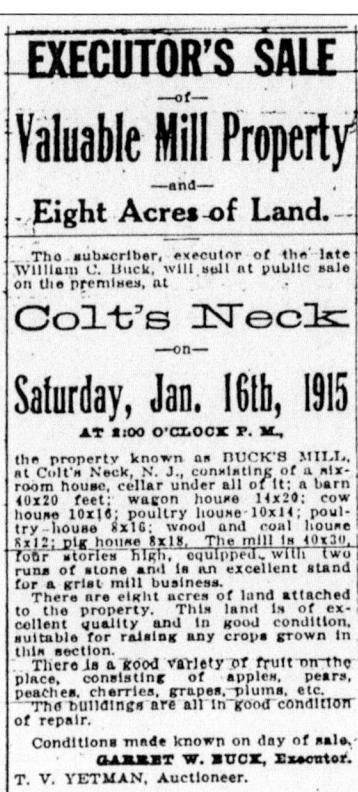

William Buck bought in 1871 the mill which stayed in the family until modern times. The ad for the 1915 estate sale gives a good description of the mill property, but by then local milling was a minor operation, flour production having been taken over by large, efficient roller mills in the Midwest. The property was bought by an heir, Alfred Buck, at the advertised sale, and by George Dittmar in c. 1948. (Special Collections & Archives, Rutgers University Libraries.)

A contemporary aerial photograph depicts the layout of the Probasco house, the centerpiece of a property now known as Duck Hollow Farm, located on the west side of Bucks Mill Road. The house (right), dating from the third quarter of the 18th century, is named for Joseph Probasco, a 19th-century owner of the mill (left). The barn, dating from the second half of the 19th century, is the major outbuilding of a complex which also includes a tenant house, shed, and ice house. The present owners, George and Florence Dittmar, have enrolled the property in the New Jersey farmland preservation program, selling the development rights to assure that the space remains open.

The mill was motor-operated in its later years, but George Dittmar wanted to restore water power. He obtained available plans for a 10-foot wheel from the Historic American Buildings Survey, had his carpenter Everett Matthews enlarge them to 28 feet, solved lumber acquisition and treatment (creosote) problems and had Matthews build the wheel, not certain it would fit. It did. The mill was destroyed in an incendiary fire in 1972, but the wheel was saved. It is seen here c. 1982 and looks similar today.

Windy Hill Farm on Laird Road, as seen here in the early 1950s, is typical of the Colts Neck farming tradition. It contains an old house on expansive grounds with outbuildings and a track

for horse-raising operations. (The Dorn's Collection.)

Henry Ellis was a 19th-century owner of a sizable farm in northern Colts Neck. The house was expanded over time from its two-story origins in the center of this c. 1930s image. The Ellis family sold the farm to William and Jesse Sweetland in 1936, who sold it to Leroy and Gladys French the following year; the buyers attached the name Plumbroke to the property. They began a series of modernizations that in recent years culminated in the place being made comfortable for modern living by building its amenities around its preserved historic core.

The Ellis house contains a late-19th-century addition in the section at right in the image at the top of the page, one obscured by trees. Its first floor contains the blue room, a finely finished room containing this fireplace surrounded by old blue tiles.

Farming at the former Henry Ellis place continued into the mid-20th-century, but the farm structures have been replaced by development.

An example of land use in zones requiring 10 acres is indicated by this aerial view of Warrenton Lane. The house lots are of smaller size, but the surrounding woodland is dedicated to maintaining the 10-acre requirement.

The Charles Haight house on the south side of County Highway 537, east of Highway 34, belonged to a wealthy businessman engaged in 19th-century trade with the Orient.

Contemporary remodeling has obscured the historic appearance of 291 County Highway 537 (south side).

The Williamson-Sickles house, one of the oldest in western Colts Neck, sits well behind School Road East. It was built in two sections, the western three bays dating from the mid-18th century, while the two eastern bays were added in the mid-19th century, the whole appearing as symmetrical house.

This house, once on the south side of County Highway 537, east of Hominy Hill Road, was prominent during the ownership of Armand Hammer. The former seat of his famed Shadow Isle Farms was demolished c. 1980s.

James L. Shearer, owner and manager of Newark radio station WHBI, bought in 1943 a 15-acre farm estate on the north side of County Highway 537, near the Tinton Falls border, which contained a house built c. 1898 by John E. Beckman. Shearer, who was also a singer, named the place Shear-Wood. He was known for his benefactions to orphaned and crippled children. The place, still recognizable, is seen on a c. 1950 postcard. (Collection of John Rhody.)

Murray M. Rosenberg purchased the large, old Atlantic Stock Farm in 1936, one absent a main house as it had been destroyed by fire c. 1920. The New Yorker, who owned controlling interest in Miles shoes, built a fine Colonial Revival house and improved the farm buildings, renaming the place Dorbrook Farm, which was referred to as a "show estate" the following year. Dorbrook attained fame for raising Murray Greys, a premier breed of beef cattle. One former owner was Harry Mc Cormick, who provided quarters for a couple of years to Gene Tunney. The gym in which he trained also burned. Monmouth County acquired the 380 acre estate in 1985 for Dorbrook Park. This post-fire aerial view is c. 1950s. (The Dorn's Collection.)

The Conover-Crine house at 60 Conover Road, once part of Daniel G. Coevenhoven's Holly Bush Farm, originated with one small section at right, one story when built, perhaps in the late 18th century. The Greek Revival main house, with fine Italianate scroll brackets, was built in the mid-19th century. The house, now on a 2-acre lot, was once the seat of a sizable farm. Henry Crine Jr. sold much of the surrounding property for development, a school, and a firehouse.

The Coevenhoven house and farm at 100 Conover Road originated with one of the township's oldest families.

Preparation for a crop-dusting flight is viewed at Colts Neck in the early 1940s. The photograph was taken by W. Edmund Kemble, born 1907 in the Burlington County pine barren area. Ed's career was in the landscape business, with an avocation in art and photography, including extensive work in color slides from the earliest days (late 1930s) of Kodachrome.

Crop dusting was and is a dangerous occupation and its applications could be indiscriminate. A principal theme in Ed Kemble's photography was disappearing aspects of New Jersey, especially rural life. He lectured extensively with his slides, before it was a popular pursuit of the many, injecting personal experience into many New Jersey topics that the following generation could only study. Ed is retired now, living in Ocean Township.

Arnold Conover preserved this scene on Uncle Fred Conover's farm, now the site of Township Hall. Horse Beauty is leading, from left to right, Fred's son Carlton, Arnold, and Fred's sister Mildred.

The farm children appear quite nattily attired on Brookside Farm, c. 1920s. From left to right are Malcolm Minton, Mildred Conover, and Arnold Conover.

The Thomas Ryall house at 204 County Highway 537 West (the south side) is a two-story Italianate hipped-roof structure built *c.* 1870. It was apparently built from plans published in Samuel Sloan's 1852 *The Model Architect*.

The Ryall house stands well preserved. There is no indication if the cupola in the image at top was ever present.

Ryall outbuildings were sold as separate residences when the property was sub-divided.

The late 1990s demolition of the house on the east side of Highway 34 across from Delicious Orchards removed one of the few remaining evidences of old farm existence on that stem of road. The barns were taken down earlier, their memory preserved by this c. 1920s image which shows Harold Gunther (left) and his brother William.

A Colts Neck farm was likely the site for Howell photographer A. Merriman's unidentified c. 1911 potato harvesting scene. Monmouth was one of the top producing counties in the nation and Colts Neck was heavily planted in potatoes. The period was critical in developing crop yields. Farmers, who had mechanized their operations over the past two decades, were applying more fertilizer, realizing that the added cost of fertilizer would be rewarded handsomely in crop yield. Prices were high and farmers prosperous, a condition that would soon change.

William and Richard Flock are seen in front of the noted Flock Farm barns. Their father, Charles, who owned the Thomas Henry Grant place in Middletown Township, bought a 120-acre farm on today's Highway 34 from the John Statesir estate in 1923.

Marion Van Dorn Flock displayed collectibles in June 1976, a time when she was one of 23 native residents honored by the township's bicentennial committee. She reminisced about life on a 400-acre farm prior to electrification, of pre-mechanized agricultural work requiring temporary help—she assisted with asparagus bunching, of education in a one-room school, and social life centered around church activities.

The January 1987 Flock Farm auction marked the end of an era. Houses now "grew" on the Flock Farm.

Robert Brennan's Due Process Stables was a nationally prominent stud farm in the 1980s. Old farms totaling about 400 acres on the south side of County Highway 537 were acquired, combined, and equipped with breeding facilities. Existing farm structures were incorporated when practicable. Due Process included a stud barn, breeding shed, mare stable, and a training center.

This 1984 image is the courtyard area of the former Bernadotte Farm. Due Process was acquired by the De Gennaro family and builder Matthew Clemente in 1996. The Estates at Due Process was planned, a series of custom-built houses surrounding a John Miller-designed 18-hole championship golf course.

The procession of cars on the south side of County Highway 537 during Decembers in the 1980s appeared to be lured by the Pied Piper of Christmas, but the attraction, the Due Process Christmas display, was better. The crèche, the calliope, the lights, and the displays added an almost magical aura to the Colts Neck holiday scene. This line-up was on December 16, 1983.

This Due Process Stable crèche was photographed in December 1982. The gate where so many passed through is now the entrance to the golf course. Visitors were handed a small card of greeting on entering. Distributed by the thousands for years, will they be a collectable of the 21st century?

John Statesir founded the Atlantic Farm in 1884; his family held the property until it was purchased by Michael Riordan, a notably successful Irish immigrant who had tenanted the place for nine years. The Scobeyville estate had been renamed Colonial Farms by the time it was sold by Howard C. Davis to John Fieramosca in 1950, who is seen with two of his horses on the stock farm he continues to run.

Fieramosca is seen in his office in 1985 with some of his many awards and momentos from his career with horses.

Five
ORGANIZATIONS

Colts Neck Fire Company Number 1 was founded in 1927. They bought a former blacksmith's shop on the south side of County Highway 537 and adapted it as their first home. It served as such for 26 years and is now the Colts Neck Honey Shop. The members pictured c. 1940 are, from left to right, as follows: (seated) Frank Demarest, Clarence Willett, Daniel Riordan, Arthur Soffel, Charles Conover, Albert Coon, John Sutphin, Louis Plotkin, Frank Magee, George Richdale, and William Hardy; (standing) Charles Crine, Raymond Walling, Fred Hill, Martin "Pop" Riley, Louis Snyder, Assistant Chief Edwin "Pat" Sherman, Chief Harold "Jake" Gunther, John Riley, Joseph Crine, Fred Perrotti, George Illmensee Sr., and Warren Snedeker. Jack Maher is seated in the truck.

The Colts Neck Fire Company and its Ladies Auxiliary held a Southern minstrel show on April 24, 1947, as a one-time fund-raising event, in the township's elementary school. Felix Santangelo directed the show, while Max Lewis handled musical arrangements and was the accompanist. The setting was a hay loft, with varied farm equipment decorating the set. Pictured is the interlocutor, Chriney Conover, who was known as "Parson" that night. He also had a musical number entitled "Pray For the Lights To Go Out."

The ladies were well represented in the April 24, 1947 minstrel show. Bertha Conover (left) and Dorothy Guenther were members of the chorus and had solo numbers. Bertha sang "Five Foot Two," while Dorothy treated the crowd to "You Broke the Only Heart That Ever Loved You."

The bicentennial year of 1976 was an exciting one at the Colts Neck Firemen's Fair. Live entertainment was added and Robert Maddox's 1923 Ahrens-Fox fire engine was on display. Posing aside it are Chairman of the Fair George Illmensee Jr. (left) and Fair Advisor Joseph Wilson.

The rides in the background have long been a staple at the Colts Neck Firemen's Fair. The foreground would have been a perfect reflection if the riders kept the boat still. However, a short sail is preferable to a perfect pose while having fun at the fair. This is a Scott Longfield photograph.

The cornerstone of the original St. Mary's Roman Catholic Church on Heyers Mill Road was laid on August 17, 1879. The 30-by-55-foot brick Gothic Revival edifice with terra-cotta ornamentation, designed by Monmouth County architect-carpenter-farmer Austin H. Patterson, was blessed by Bishop Michael A. Corrigan on November 23, 1879. This building, having served as a church until replaced by the present St. Mary's in 1972, was sold for use as a private residence. The image is from a c. 1905 postcard. (Collection of Michael F. Bremer.)

A 60-pound fiberglass statue of the Blessed Virgin Mary was hoisted into place at the present St. Mary's Church at the northeast corner of Highway 34 and Phalanx Road on August 29, 1972. Ground had been broken in December 1971; the church was completed in 1972 and dedicated by Bishop George Ahr on on February 11, 1973, a month after St. Mary's pastor, Father Raymond Griffin, died unexpectedly at age 48. The statue is still in place and the grounds enhanced by a number of other structures, notably a 1980 spiritual center.

George W. Ahr, born 1904 in Newark and a graduate of Seton Hall, completed seminary studies at the North American College in Rome, Italy, and was ordained a priest in 1928 in the chapel of Leonine College, also in Rome. After brief parish work, Ahr began an academic career, his principal experience prior to his consecration as the seventh bishop of the Diocese of Trenton in 1950. He served until 1979, longer than any bishop in the diocese, dying in 1993. Bishop Ahr is seen visiting the old St. Mary's for confirmation c. 1956.

The earliest worship in Colts Neck was held through the assistance of traveling clergy and later by meeting in non-church buildings. Efforts to organize a church in Colts Neck begun c. 1848 failed due to insufficient funds. A second effort in 1853 succeeded. The cornerstone of the Reformed Church was laid in the fall of 1854 and the Greek Revival edifice, erected by Long Branch contractor Ebenezer G. Goltra (architect unknown), was completed in 1855. Formal organization followed in 1856 and the first pastor, the Rev. Jacob S. Wyckoff, was installed that August. This c. 1903 image of the church on the north side of County Highway 537, west of Highway 34, depicts a building little-changed today, although the steeple was lowered in 1900. Later changes include a 1906 Sunday school addition and the 1911 installation of stain-glass windows. (Collection of Michael F. Bremer.)

Architect-carpenter Austin H. Patterson built this parsonage for the Colts Neck Reformed Church in 1857, using as a model Design VII for a symmetrical cottage in A.J. Downing's important work *The Architecture of Country Houses*. The place, still standing on the north side of County Highway 537, is now a private residence, its integrity compromised by repairs following a c. 1992 fire. (Collection of Michael F. Bremer.)

The store and post office was located on the west side of Heyers Mill Road at Vanderburg, an old village founded as Edinburg in the 18th century, one still retaining a 19th-century character. The post office was founded in 1883, but was discontinued in 1918. The subjects, unknown, may include the storekeeper. The image is a c. 1911 Merriman photographic postcard.

Garret R. Thompson delivered mail for the Colts Neck post office from 1962 to 1982. He discovered a birds nest on the south side of County Highway 537, west of Five Points Road, necessitating alternate drop-off arrangements while eggs or young birds were present.

The former Atlantic Township Hall was built on the south side of County Highway 537, west of Heyers Mill Road, in 1909. It is viewed in an election day image from the late 1940s, with a partial view of the town's World War II honor roll at left.

The present Colts Neck Hall was built overlooking a pond facing Cedar Drive in 1964. It was designed by Red Bank architect Bernard Kellenyi, a contemporary expression of traditional Georgian motifs. Kellenyi, whose oeuvre generally has a modern character, spent a week in Williamsburg, Virginia, absorbing early American design. The building was intended as the core of a new township center.

The 1964 New Jersey State Police barracks, also a Georgian design by Bernard Kellenyi, was an addition to the Colts Neck township center. The local state police, formerly located in an old residence in Shrewsbury, were needful of modern facilities. Colts Neck had no municipal force then, but possessed the space for the required building, facilitating the match. The township's police now occupy the building, along with its municipal court.

The former Grange Hall on Heyers Mill Road was remodeled for library use in 1982. This image is from the library's dedication on June 12. The building is still used as a library, its entrance altered for use as a handicapped ramp. A campaign for a much-needed new library is active as this book goes to press in the summer of 1998.

Franklin Ellis' 1885 *History of Monmouth County* indicates early education in Colts Neck was conducted in a house a 1/2 mile west of the village, citing an old-timer's (Charles Bowman) memory of having attended there as early as 1813. The house served until this fine Greek Revival-style building was erected in 1856. Located on the north side of County Highway near the Reformed church, the school stands remodeled beyond recognition as a residence. (Collection of Michael F. Bremer.)

The Scobeyville school was built on the north side of County Highway 537, east of Laird Road in 1851. It, too, replaced a private residence as a place of instruction. The Scobeyville school demonstrated the difficulty of Colts Neck's late arrival at school consolidation. The school was closed early in September 1920, unable to hire a teacher at $900 per year, necessitating the intervention of the Reformed minister as a volunteer teacher. The building, sold in 1923 and remodeled in 1924 into a home for the families of William Carter and Walter Oakes, was also believed to have been used as a store. It is believed to have been destroyed at an unspecified date. (Collection of Michael F. Bremer.)

According to Ellis, the Vanderberg school was built prior to 1836 at the southeast corner of Conover and Heyers Mill Road, and rebuilt in 1865; the extension in front appears to be a later addition. It was remodeled as a private residence c. 1920, but was still readily recognizable from this c. 1911 Merriman photographic postcard.

The Montrose School, built c. 1860s, was the last of the early Colts Neck one-room schools, and it stood vacant for a long while at Montrose Road and Cedar Drive. Its rehabilitation for historical use was an early restoration project of the Colts Neck Historical Society. It is seen at the project's October 1971 dedication.

Colts Neck was late in consolidating its local one-room schools. Proposals for a new school were voted down repeatedly, but a 1922 effort was successful, resulting in the construction of a six-room brick school on the south side of County Highway 537, east of Highway 34 on a lot bought from Warren Matthews. Later additions were built in the rear, including a large, one-story wing designed by J. Hallam Conover added to the southwest in 1950. Replaced by modern schools, this building once housed township school administrative offices and is now the Meridian Academy, an alternative school for emotionally disturbed and neurologically impaired students between the ages of 5 and 21.

At right are Bertha Hickey and Arnold Conover, together with an unidentified classmate in a 1932 play at the Atlantic Elementary School. The two married after a 10-year courtship and still fondly recollect the presentation, although neither its name nor their fellow player.

When asked what she was doing amidst the male students, Dorothy Decher Gunther quickly quipped, "I was always with the boys," before offering a practical answer that she photographed the girls of the 1929 Atlantic Township Elementary School graduating class. To her right in the photograph at left are Pat Sherman and a boy named Dominick. Frank and John are to her left. The girls in the photograph at right are, in front from left to right, Betty Matthews, an unidentified girl, and one named Mary. In back are Sadie Mack, Cora Douglas, probably Olga Schwenker, and Alice Hyatt.

"Look, children. We teachers are dour and disagreeable and want you students to appear so, too" could have been the posing instructions to this unidentified class, c. 1900. The building appears to be the Colts Neck school.

Henry Dickson Mercer, who founded the steamship company States Marine Corp. around 1930, began buying farms near Hominy Hill c. 1940, accumulating hundreds of acres. Mercer, who lived in Rumson, developed a prize-winning herd of Guernsey and Charolais cattle at his farm, named for its section in Colts Neck. He was an enthusiastic yachtsman and golfer; a barn became remodeled for use as a clubhouse for the private golf course he built on the farm.

The 7,059-yard, par 72 championship course was designed for tournament play by the noted Robert Trent Jones and built in 1964. Its restricted, private access gave it an aura of mystery. The most repeated lore of its origin was Mercer's anger at the rebuff of Japanese business guests at a local club. Mercer became ill late in life and it has been said he never played a full round at his course. The County of Monmouth bought the course and property in 1976 and now operates the facility as a public course. Mercer died at his home in Lyford Cay, Nassau, at the age of 84 in 1978.

Six
PEOPLE, PLACES, EVENTS

Sidney Martin, born 1920, combined two careers for many years; he was a meat broker by day and an artist in his leisure hours. He worked in various media. Although Sid painted early in his career, he is best known for his sculpture. He went through other stylistic phases before creating the idea of large blown fiberglass pieces of semi-abstract figures, often in action or contemplative poses. *Portrait of the Reader* captures the spirit of the latter. The 6-by-5-by-6-foot figure is in the Colts Neck sculpture garden of noted collectors Howard and Frances Schoor. Sid died on April 26, 1996, but the world is brighter for the art he left.

The date of origin of the Colts Neck Inn at the northeast corner of County Highway 537 and Heyers Mill Road is generally regarded as 1717. The hotel was a major public gathering place in colonial times, serving as a site for agitation in an area hotly contested between forces loyal to the crown and rebellious patriots. The image is a c. 1911 Merriman photo postcard.

Samuel Laird, a notable 19th-century owner of the Colts Neck Inn who established a distillery elsewhere on the premises, bought the place in 1812 with partner Joseph H. Van Mater, buying the latter's interest in 1828. This c. 1914 image shows the Monmouth County Hunt gathered in front during the tenure of Lewis Snyder, whose first day of ownership featured various festivities including a trotting race from Colts Neck to Long Branch.

The inn long ago ceased being a hotel, but was widely known as a restaurant. A major modern extension built on the east is seen in 1963, while the original building maintained its integrity. Subsequent alterations have left the old structure unrecognizable. The establishment discarded one of the oldest and most historic names of Monmouth County hospitality, renaming the restaurant in the summer of 1997. (The Dorn's Collection.)

The ambiance of Colts Neck village during the 1950s was little changed from a century earlier. County Highway 537 is seen here in a view looking east. (Special Collections & Archives, Rutgers University Libraries.)

Heyers Mill Road is seen looking north c. 1911 in a Merriman postcard. (Collection of Michael F. Bremer.)

Heyers Saw Mill on Yellow Brook at Heyers Mill Road reportedly dated from at least from c. 1800; seen here in the early 20th century, the structure was periodically enlarged and rebuilt. Ownership included Haights, Conovers, and a Dr. Cook, who sold it to John Heyer. John's son Frank owned the mill at the time of Monmouth County's most tragic mill accidents. (Collection of Shrewsbury Historical Society.)

Chunks of ice, loosened and broken by a freshet (flood) threatened the mill dam at Heyers Saw Mill in February 1902. Heyer and seven helpers were attempting to save the dam on the night of the 28th by breaking-up the ice and getting it over the dam, when the dam broke, sweeping six of them into the water. They were battered by ice chunks and timbers in the ensuing torrent. Four were killed. Heyer, uninjured, rebuilt the dam, seen here in a *c.* 1911 image by A. Merriman. That storm was long a standard of measure for local storm severity. The mill is long gone; the property was sold by his family to Theodore Rowe in 1922 to settle Heyer's estate. (Collection of Michael F. Bremer.)

The Daniel Rezeau Conover home was built *c.* 1863 at 180 Heyers Mill Road.

The Colts Neck Cash Store that formerly stood on the northwest corner of County Highway 537 and Heyers Mill Road is viewed on a Merriman postcard c. 1911. The place burned at an unspecified date early in the century; a house built on the site preserves the arched window on its east elevation. (Collection of Michael F. Bremer.)

The Colts Neck General Store, founded in 1858 by Levi Scobey, entered modern times with the character of an old country establishment carrying a wide variety of diverse merchandise. It is viewed in the early 1940s, its sign covering attic windows and with no-longer-present gas pumps in front. The exterior as seen in this image is readily recognizable today, but the interior has been remodeled into a deli-convenience store; it is now owned by Ronnie Green. (A.W. Edmund Kemble photograph.)

This Merriman c. 1911 postcard image is likely County Highway 537 looking east from a point west of Highway 34, at a time about two decades prior to the construction of the latter road. (Collection of Michael F. Bremer.)

Harry Barth is seen in 1986 in his Colts Neck Honey Shop, one of the town's best-known landmarks. It occupies a building that formerly served as the firehouse and a blacksmith's shop on the south side of County Highway 537. Barth, a resident in the township since the late 1940s, is a charter member of the Colts Neck First Aid Squad.

Walter R. Voorhees, born in 1923, resided 40 years in Colts Neck, a spell embracing long community service. He was a member of the Old Brick Reformed Church and its Greater Consistory. Voorhees was the recipient of the Boy Scouts of America Silver Beaver award, having served as a scoutmaster for 33 years. He took special pleasure in Revolutionary War commemorative activities, was a member of the Associated Regiments of the American Revolution, and was the founder of the Joshua Huddy Company of Fife and Drummers. A Marine recipient of the Bronze Star in World War II, Voorhees is pictured in 1977, in a blue-and-white Continental soldier's uniform which he made. He died in 1992.

A favorite informal measure of the effects of a drought was eyeing the water level of the Swimming River Reservoir. Dry, indeed, was the summer of 1981, as evidenced by this image taken on Muhlenbrink Road. While shallow at this point, the reservoir's deep water can and does pose a safety hazard.

Ann (Mrs. William) Miles, a former postmaster, was a longtime Colts Neck historian and the principal force on the committee that produced the 1964 booklet *History of Colts Neck*. The Mileses, also active in the restoration of the Montrose School, moved to Virginia following retirement, where he became chief of his Native American tribe.

Arnold Conover decided to test his memory by recalling fellow members of the Colts Neck Holiday Gun Club who posed at their clubhouse off Heulitt Road on May 30, 1931. They are, from left to right, as follows: (front row) Stanley Hunt, William Hunt, Harry Pullen, John Sutphin, A. Simmonds, Chriney Conover, Joe Phillips, Alfred Buck, Ray Walling, Garrett W. Buck, Lewis Snyder, Ray Holling, and Rezeau Conover; (back row) Frank Magee, John Grant, Newell Van Dorn, Walter Conover, Clarence Willett, George Richdale, Charles Flock, Al Black, Willard Magee, Charles Bennett, Russell Heulitt, Clarence Heiser, Winsor Heulitt, Spafford Walling, Howard Buck, Arnold Conover, Jack Lawrence, and George Hayes.

George and Amelia Decher lived in this still-standing house on the corner of Creamery Road and County Highway 537, moving from Newark in the 1920s. He was the first Colts Neck fire chief.

The Decher produce stand was adjacent on the east to their house (pictured at the top of the page). The stand is shown here c. 1930s, a time when roadside stands dotted the popular country road (today #537) running from Freehold to Eatontown. The Dechers later built a store east of the stand, which has been remodeled into a residence owned by their daughter, Dorothy Gunther, lender of the image.

Harold "Jake" Gunther (right) and his friend Joline appear quite pleased over the success of their deer hunt. They are pictured c. 1960s at the former's home.

"Rocky," the life-sized fiberglass horse that long-decorated the premises of the Colts Neck Studio Shop, an antiques place on the north side of County Highway 537, east of Highway 34, had two principal effects. The unfamiliar could be startled by the "creature" appearing to be leaping a fence, while many road regulars regarded it with affection, as a quirky neighborhood decoration, which was not bad considering its ugliness. Seen in 1983, it is gone now; a neighbor does not recall when. The author's preference for roadside incongruity, however, was the live camel (see p. 65).

Dorothy Decher Gunther is seen on County Highway 537 in 1930, near her father Conrad's store, located west of the gas pump. The photographer's violation of portrait posing convention (with a competing background) provides us with a fine view of that road looking east just prior to the start of its change of character from working agriculture to gentlemen's farms.

The Laird's Distillery baseball team is seen in a 1934 image, about the time Harold "Jake" Gunther began his near-50-year career there. He is at left in the middle row.

Perhaps the author's fascination with Maryann's Inn dating from his 1971 arrival in the county stems from the incongruity of an old-style roadhouse in the midst of gentlemen's farms. Located at the northeast corner of County Highway 537 and Muhlenbrink Road, the building dates from Scobeyville's working agrarian past, its age suggested by a stone foundation and tree trunk posts. Maryann, dating from the 1940s, was Maryann Malyski, daughter of owner John Malyski. The exterior image is instantly recognizable, as change has been subtle. The interior has been extensively altered, however. The images are c. 1950, the date suggested, in part, by the small television with the program announcement advertising wrestling (yuck!). Some things change; Laurie Genke announced that pizza is popular now.

Carroll Barclay bought William Lerch's nearly-100-acre Delicious Fruit Farm in the early 1920s. The farm was reported in 1924 to grow 12 varieties of apples. Much of the output was trucked to Newark for sale. Lerch built a 48-by-96-foot cold storage warehouse in 1921 to facilitate his operation. Barclay is seen inspecting his apples in an image earlier seen in the December 1937 *Monmouth Pictorial*.

Barclay's apple orchard expanded into retail sales in 1960, a then-novel operation for a local grower, at this modest stand by their fields on the north side of County Highway 537. Early publicity included a postcard with a printed message announcing 200 acres of orchards and their own fruit pies (see p. 118). This image was taken in August 1960. (The Dorn's Collection.)

Carroll Barclay's apple trees provided pleasant spring blossoms. They are seen in an image from the spring 1939 *Monmouth Pictorial*, their appeal enhanced by county beauties Jane Guptil, Barbara Mc Clees, and Charlotte Mount.

Carroll Barclay Jr. transformed his plantings to dwarf or semi-dwarf trees, increasing greatly the number of trees per acre and facilitating spraying, pruning, and picking. Buyers' taste was addressed by grafting branches of favored apples to trunks of less-popular varieties.

Apple packing is viewed in 1976 during Carroll Barclay's ownership of Delicious Orchards. He was proud of their stature as the only merchants who grew, peeled and baked their own apples into pie. Much of the apple harvest went into cider (opposite) or retail sale. Delicious Orchards' large produce department sells local fruit and vegetables in season and an extensive selection year-round from other markets as well.

Janet Barclay supplemented the new retail stand by baking pies in her own oven, perhaps a dozen or so for Sunday sales. Overwhelming success was immediate. Soon a commercial oven in her home was needed. Janet started with a family recipe, adapting it for commercial production by extrapolating ingredient quantities. Several varieties are baked, but it is the apple pie more than any other product that earned Delicious Orchards regional fame. Author's tip: Apple pies baked in late summer-early fall from green apples have a delicious tart bite unlike any other he has experienced. This image is from 1976.

Cider was a product of the early stand. Although apples are blended, taste may vary from time-to-time, depending on the current mix. At the time of this 1976 image of the packing operation, Delicious Orchards pressed 40,000 bushels of apples per year for the 125,000 gallons then sold at the store annually.

Merriman photographic postcards provide stunning glimpses of the c. 1910 landscape. Their locales are rarely labeled, so identification depends on recognizable landmarks (or hand-written messages). This image is County Highway 537, probably east of Highway 34. It was known as the turnpike, usually the Freehold-Eatontown Turnpike, long after the County acquired the road. (Collection of John Rhody.)

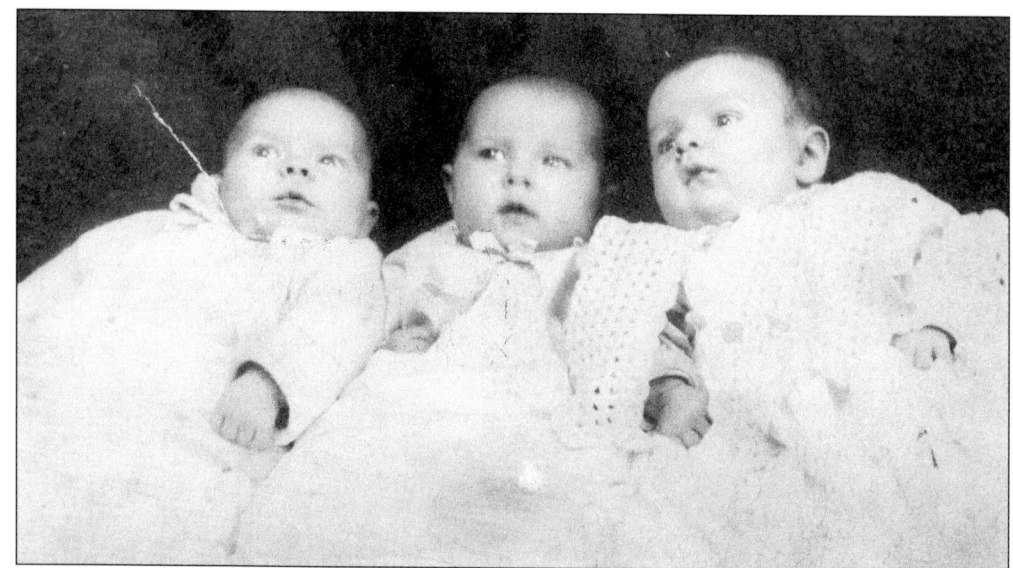

Sibling rivalry is well recognized, but cousin rivalry can be even more competitive. After all, the mothers do not have to live with the other competing youngsters. Arnold Conover (left) is seen with Fred Conover's son Carlton (center) and Herbert Conover's daughter Elizabeth, the three born within a one-week period in 1911. Arnold is the only survivor and he did not tell who talked or walked first.

Mildred and Arnold Conover are seen c. 1920. Perhaps their apparent displeasure stems from being over-dressed.

Gladys and Orland Grant provide a charming mother and child portrait c. 1920s.

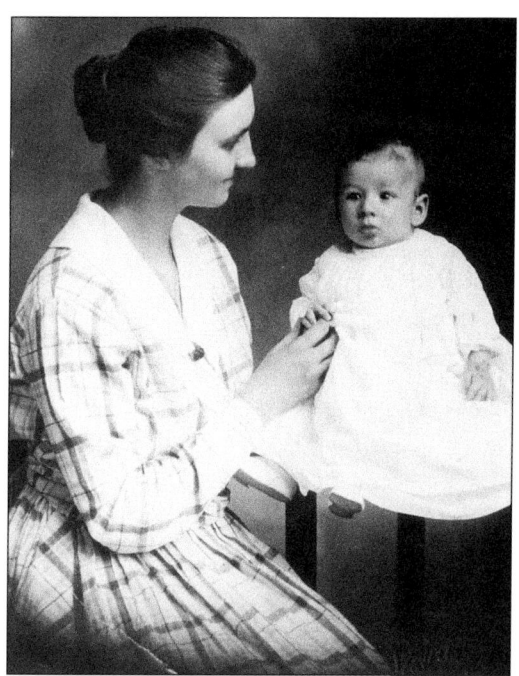

Jim Gary was born in 1939 in Florida and raised in Colts Neck, where he began his Iron Butterfly Art Studio and Gallery. Gary became best known for sculptures formed by welding automobile parts, typically as dinosaurs (see the author's *Red Bank, Vol. I*, p. 80). He is seen in 1971 with an important early work, *Universal Woman*, a female torso fashioned from hundreds of ordinary automobile washers, for which he won the James V. Herring Award and $500 at that year's National Black Artists Exhibition in Washington, D.C.

The Monmouth County Hunt, an organization consisting primarily of Rumson and Middletown Township country estate owners, held drag hunting events at various nearby farming locales. A trio of unidentified members and their dogs were photographed early in this century while preparing for a Colts Neck hunt.

Frederick Moog Jr. was a boating enthusiast in his later years, rising to commander of the Shrewsbury Power Squadron. He was a skilled equestrian as a young man and is seen with his mount c. 1930s at an unidentified Colts Neck locale. Moog was also a polo player.

The Colts Neck Creamery, on a branch of Yellow Brook at Creamery Road near County Highway 537, was founded by Thomas and Peter Walling of Shrewsbury, who utilized the former Snyder Grist Mill (believed to have founded in the 19th century by Christopher Probasco). The Wallings sold to Asbury Park interest in 1903 and are believed to have begun a creamery in the village. Farmers selling excess milk to creameries was then regarded as a profitable alternative to raising calves. There is no known trace of the dam or mill. (Collection of Michael F. Bremer.)

Instances of heavy aircraft traffic over Colts Neck can be attributed to the Phalanx Road location of this VOR (Very high-frequency Omni-directional Receiver), a navigational aid. The device's transmitting and receiving radio signals, sent to and received from nearby aircraft, permit pilots to ascertain their position, as they know the fixed locations of the VORs around their flight paths.

The Vanderburg blacksmith's shop on Heyers Mill Road is seen in a *c.* 1911 Merriman photographic postcard. The structure still stands, remodeled as a private residence.

Photographer A. Merriman found two youngsters to add a human element to his *c.* 1911 view of Heyers Mill Road looking north in Vanderberg. The former school (see p. 99) is on the right.

An 18th-century house on the southwest corner of Heyers Mill Road and Indian Trail appears to have origins with the Conover family. It was bought in 1939 by Dr. Walter J. Anderson, who expanded and modernized the place, then the seat of a 15-acre farm. The house was named Chestnut Rise in the 1950s for the presence of a 19th-century Asian chestnut tree. Development now surrounds the house. The image is from the current ownership of Jan and Richard Napoliello Jr.

Virginia Amend, born and raised in Newark, lived in California before returning to New Jersey. She and her husband, James, have lived on an old farm for 40 years, purchasing the place when it still had an outhouse. Virginia has witnessed not only change in Colts Neck's residential fabric, but also its social composition and political ethic from her unique perspective there of an independent journalistic voice. She has published the Colts Neck Calendar for 27 years, earning stature as the "Conscience of Colts Neck." Virginia points out her business career tracks the rise of women in contemporary society. The Monmouth College graduate is prideful of educating three daughters in substantial colleges, from a working-class background during a period paralleling her own education. Virginia's publication is an open forum for three constituencies of readers, small businesses, and her charities. Her independent voice has brought vocal and strenuous clashes with Colts Neck officialdom, but she looks at attempts to silence her with an esteem comparable to battle stars. The image dates from 1972.

The chicken coops formerly located north of Clover Hill Road reflect the early working agricultural character of Colts Neck. They were demolished in the mid-1960s for the construction of Clover Hill Estates.

Williamsburg North, begun in the mid-1960s by Walter Zimmerer, was the first of the major housing developments in Colts Neck.

The street Fairway East/West was built by Walter Zimmerer around the old Kline house, seen here in a 1965 image from Vanderburg Road.

The Raleighs have long been an active Colts Neck couple. Jim, a retired Bell engineer, is deeply involved in Revolutionary War, cartographic, and genealogical historical circles. He is seen in 1976 with his first flash into Monmouth history, the Revolutionary War signal beacon erected on County Highway 520, on the Holmdel side of the Colts Neck border. His wife, Frances (in the foreground), was editor of the *Know Your Township-Colts Neck* booklet, and is seen at the time of its 1976 publication, in an image with Mary Doherty, then president of the League of Women Voters of Holmdel-Colts Neck.

The rumor that the 1950s roadside eatery staple Chicken in the Basket had as its origin the canine classic of *Kitten in the Basket* is totally untrue. This quartet of four-legged friends was photographed in Colts Neck in the 1920s.

What a way to go, via goat cart, the author's classic closing. This occasion has an appealing handler, Dorothy Decher Gunther, seen *c.* 1930. She recalls the cart was used around their farm for recreational purposes. So long until Volume II.